HOW TO SECURE YOUR PRIVATE DATA ON FACEBOOK

Step by step guide to managing how other apps access your Facebook data

Samuel MOORE

TABLE OF CONTENTS

CHAPTER ONE

1.1 Security Overview

Most likely you are reading this book because there has been a data leak or breach or you have heard about some data breach on Facebook or some other social media site or app, and you are concerned about how this impacts you and what you can do to protect your data or at least limit your exposure.

This book is intended to help you (a Facebook App user) and other Facebook app users to take pro-active actions to protect your personal data.

1.2 Why Protect Your Personal Data

Hackers and (irresponsible) organizations are attempting to grab people's data with the intention to sell it or pass it on for financial gain. The data we are talking about here are private user data such as: name, date of birth, social security numbers, bank account details, credit card details, health information, location and whatever data that can be passed on for marketing or in worst case scenarios identity theft, cloning or impersonation scams. So there is a great need for app users to be vigilant and to take proactive measures to secure their personal data.

The reason why this issue seems to be very pertinent for Facebook app users is because many other apps and sites give you the option of logging in with your Facebook account.

f Log in with Facebook

You may be familiar with the login with Facebook icon above, which you probably may have also used to log into other Apps. While this is laudable and very convenient for users, so they do not have to create separate usernames or passwords for other apps or sites they interact with, it appears this convenience is coming at a price unbeknown to the users who log in to these other apps with their Facebook credentials.

The challenge is that these third-party apps are exploiting your connection to Facebook for authentication to harvest your private data and information including in some cases your contacts without the realization of the user.

I have friends and colleagues who when we looked at their Facebook mobile app settings together were literally shocked by the number of apps that had access to their data through Facebook. In some cases, some of them claimed not to remember downloading or installing the apps that had access to this data. It may be difficult to substantiate their claims of strange apps installed on their devices, which is out of the scope of this book. The focus of this book is on Facebook and other or any apps that use Facebook authentication to gain access to user's private data.

It is also imperative to note and state here that Facebook has acted as a responsible global company to provide measures for users to limit their exposure and protect their data. However, many continue to be exposed and affected by these data leaks and breaches because they do not know what to do to safeguard their data resulting in dangerous consequences to the users in some cases.

1.3 Data Leak

April 2018, Mark Zuckerberg, The Chairman and CEO of Facebook is questioned by Congress about Facebook's handling of users data amidst the recent revelation of data leaks and unauthorized harvesting of over 50 million Facebook users private data by Cambridge Analytica.

CHAPTER TWO

2.0 Security Features and Settings

It is believed that Facebook as a responsible corporate citizen of the world will continue to do its best to protect its users, but users must avail themselves of this protection by getting to know the relevant security settings and features on Facebook and turn them on as appropriate.

We will now look into some of the Facebook App features and settings available for users to protect their private data and limit their exposure to illegal, unauthorized harvesting of their private data when they log into other Apps using Facebook.

2.1 Your Login Password

Firstly, if connecting to Facebook using a browser, check your browser and ensure you have a secure connection to the Facebook site.

Look out for the secure "https" connection in the URL or website address when connecting to Facebook.

For mobile app downloads be sure you are downloading the right app published by Facebook.

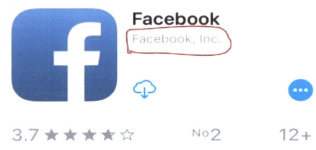

Facebook

Facebook, Inc.

3.7 ★ ★ ★ ★ ☆   No2   12+

What's New   Version History

Version 168.0   1d ago

Thanks for using Facebook! To make our app better for you, we bring updates to the App Store regularly.   more

Preview

The "Facebook, Inc." text in the snapshot above confirms the publisher of this app as Facebook Incorporated as well as other information such as the version number, the current overall or average rating of the app, the applicable age restriction, etc.

Keep your account safe by making sure to change your password often and use a "strong" password. In simple terms, a strong password is a password that is not easily guessable. It is advisable to use a password of not less than eight characters in length and should be a combination of alphabets, numbers and even special symbols e.g., @, +, *, etc.

2.2   Login Notifications and Two Factor Authentication

Login into Facebook on a browser and select settings from the dropdown arrow on the top right and click "Security and Login".

Scroll down to "Get alerts about unrecognized logins" update these settings as desired and save your changes.

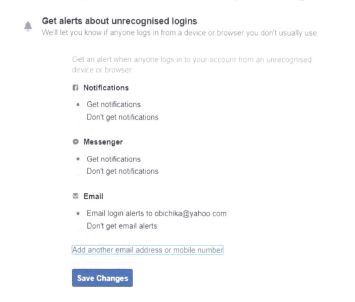

What is authentication? In very plain terms, it is the process of confirming or verifying that a user trying to access a resource is who he/she claims they are or at least that they have the consent, approval or permission of the principal benefactor or Resource Owner to operate on their behalf.

According to the SecurEnvoy website:

> "Two Factor Authentication, also known as 2FA, two step verification or TFA (as an acronym), is an extra layer of security that is known as "multi factor authentication" that requires not only a password and username but also something that only, and only, that user has on them, i.e. a piece of information only they should know or have immediately to hand - such as a physical token.
>
> Using a username and password together with a piece of information that only the user knows makes it harder for potential intruders to gain access and steal that person's personal data or identity."
>
> [www.securenvoy.com, 22 April 2018, **Retrieved from URL**:
> https://www.securenvoy.com/two-factor-authentication/what-is-2fa.shtm]

2.3 How to setup two factor authentication

Login into the Facebook site or app, click on Settings, select Security and Login, click the "Edit" button by the "Use two-factor authentication" title and click the hyperlink "setup" to specify your two-step authentication for accessing your Facebook account.

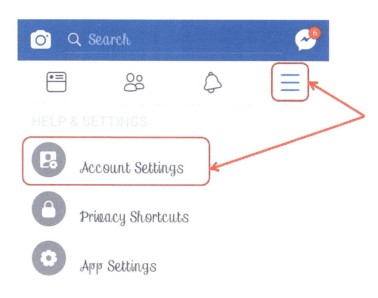

HELP & SETTINGS

Account Settings

Privacy Shortcuts

App Settings

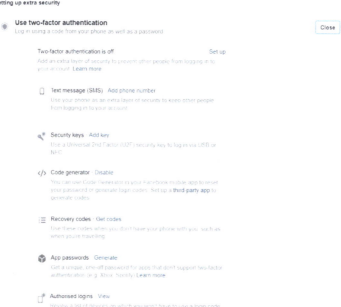

Setting up extra security

Use two-factor authentication
Log in using a code from your phone as well as a password

Close

Two-factor authentication is off · Set up
Add an extra layer of security to prevent other people from logging in to your account. Learn more

Text message (SMS) · Add phone number
Use your phone as an extra layer of security to keep other people from logging in to your account.

Security keys · Add key
Use a Universal 2nd Factor (U2F) security key to log in via USB or NFC.

Code generator · Disable
You can use Code Generator in your Facebook mobile app to reset your password or generate login codes. Set up a third-party app to generate codes.

Recovery codes · Get codes
Use these codes when you don't have your phone with you, such as when you're travelling.

App passwords · Generate
Get a unique, one-off password for apps that don't support two-factor authentication (e.g. Xbox, Spotify). Learn more

Authorised logins · View
Review a list of devices on which you won't have to use a login code.

2.4   Verify Logged in Devices and Sessions

Under account settings, take a look at the devices where your account is logged in and confirm that the devices are yours or at least familiar and that the sessions are approved by you.

Click on the three vertical dotted button to access the "LogOut" and "Not You" options. Use the "Not You" if you do not recognize the login or session and think your account has been compromised and someone may have logged into it from a different location.

Where you're logged in

Windows PC ·
Chrome   Active now

iPhone ·
Mobile Safari   4 April at 10 06

Note: Some of the snapshot images showing location of the settings may differ for different operating systems and (or) manufacturers but the links to look out for are pretty much the same.

2.5 Apps where you have logged in with Facebook

To view these apps where you have logged in using your Facebook credentials:

    i.   Click on Settings

    ii.   Select Account Settings

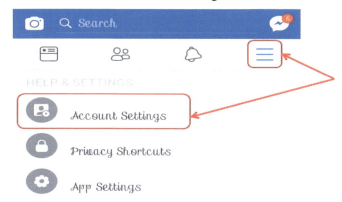

    iii.   Scroll down the list and Select **Apps**

iv.   Select "**Logged in with Facebook**" from the next
       page

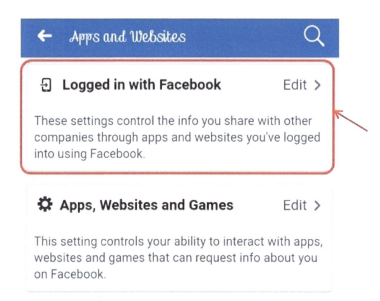

v.   Next page appears with three tabs: **Active**,
       Expired and **Removed**.

Active tab lists active apps which you have recently logged
into with Facebook.

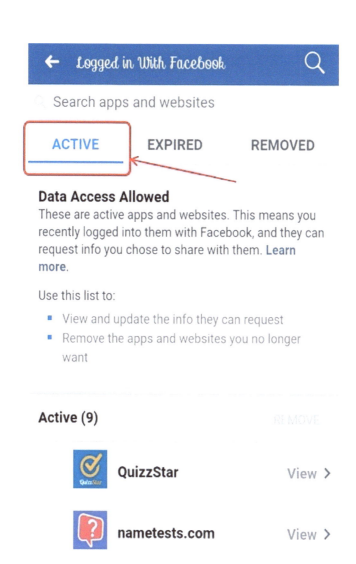

The **Expired** tab lists apps that you have logged into in the past with Facebook but because they have not been used in a while the access is now expired, and you will have to re-login to renew the access. Please note that although the access may be expired, these apps, websites or companies may still have your data (if any) which was collected when you logged in with Facebook.

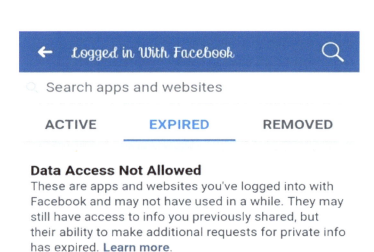

Search apps and websites

ACTIVE   **EXPIRED**   **REMOVED**

Data Access Not Allowed
These are apps and websites you've logged into with Facebook and may not have used in a while. They may still have access to info you previously shared, but their ability to make additional requests for private info has expired. **Learn more**.

You can still log into these apps and websites using Facebook.

Use this list to:

- Renew access to apps and websites
- Edit the info they can request
- Remove the apps and websites you no longer want

Expired (19)   REMOVE

TripAdvisor

The **Removed** tabs show a list of apps which you have removed their access to your Facebook data or account. Just like the Expired Apps these Apps, Websites or Organisations may still have the data you shared when their access was

Search apps and websites

ACTIVE   EXPIRED   REMOVED

Removed Apps and Websites

These are apps and websites you removed from your account. This means they may still have access to info you previously shared, but can't make additional requests for private info. This list may not include all apps and websites you've removed. **Learn more**.

Use this list to view details about your removed apps and websites.

Removed (0)

You don't have any removed apps or websites to review.

active.

vi. **Back to the Active tab**, scroll through the list of active apps that you have logged into with Facebook and select any app from the list by selecting VIEW.

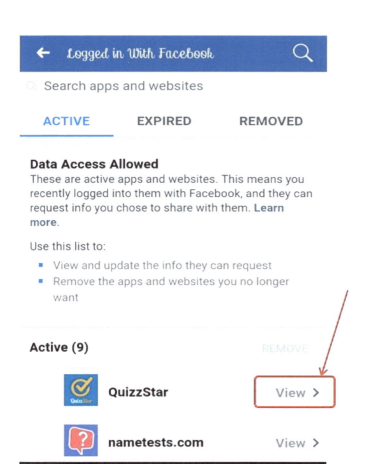

vii.   The ticked bright blue circles in the snapshot below indicate access or items on Facebook which you are sharing with the app. You can turn off sharing by un-ticking the circle. However, you will notice the circle corresponding to Public Profile is ticked and disabled. This is required by Facebook as the minimum information that will be shared with the app, and this is your public profile information.

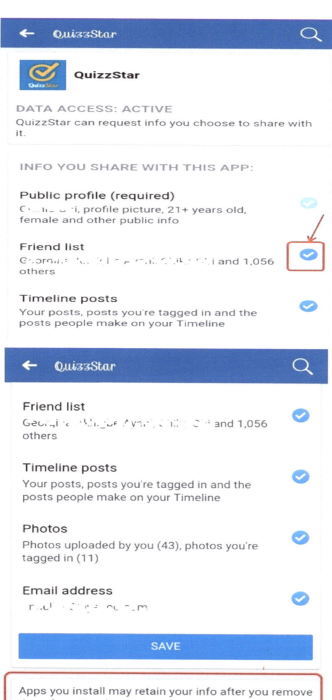

← QuizzStar 🔍

QuizzStar

DATA ACCESS: ACTIVE
QuizzStar can request info you choose to share with it.

INFO YOU SHARE WITH THIS APP:

Public profile (required)
C... .. ..i, profile picture, 21+ years old, female and other public info ✓

Friend list
G...roui.. ... . i and 1,056 others ✓

Timeline posts
Your posts, posts you're tagged in and the posts people make on your Timeline ✓

← QuizzStar 🔍

Friend list
Geor,i.. ... . and 1,056 others ✓

Timeline posts
Your posts, posts you're tagged in and the posts people make on your Timeline ✓

Photos
Photos uploaded by you (43), photos you're tagged in (11) ✓

Email address
r..ch... ... . .m ✓

SAVE

Apps you install may retain your info after you remove them from Facebook. **Contact the app developer** to remove this info.

As you can see in the snapshot above, the Quizzstar app has access to the Friends List, email address, photos uploads of this Facebook user and much more. So in this classic example, this app is not only accessing this user's data and photos, but it is overreaching to the photos of other users where this user has been tagged. Sadly, these other Facebook users may not even have this app installed on their phones and may not even know that their photos are accessible to this app.

Remember to click/tap the save button to store any changes you have made. Please as mentioned earlier, it is important to note Facebook's message encircled in red in the snapshot above.

Apps you install may retain your info after you remove them from Facebook. **Contact the app developer** to remove this info.

CHAPTER THREE

3.0   Staying Safe on Facebook

Your private data security on Facebook requires pro-active measures from both Facebook as an organization (owner and operator of the App) and you the user. So you must do your own part to complete the security circle and limit your risk and exposure.

3.1   Profile Picture Login

Facebook has a feature for logging into your account by clicking on your profile picture. While this may seem very convenient, it is not advisable to have this setting turned on for your account when using a public or shared laptop/ computer.

If you already have it turned on, for such a computer follow the steps below to turn it off.

Go to Settings >> Account Settings >> Security and Login >> Log in using your profile picture.

Click "Turn of Profile picture login".

3.2   Review your Facebook Security and Login

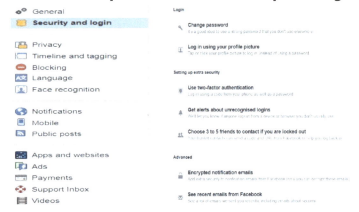

3.3   Download and Review Your Facebook Data

Log into Facebook and select the dropdown arrow and click on Settings

Click/Select General, move to the bottom/end of the right panel content to find "Download a copy of your Facebook data". Note that the Download a copy is a hyperlink. Click on this hyperlink to download your data.

If you are requesting this download for the first time then you should get an email from Facebook after you start the archive of your data for download.

Click on the "Start Archive" (to process the archive data) or Download Archive button if the archive has been processed and is available for download.

You may be required to re-enter your password to proceed with the download. This revalidation is repeated for subsequent downloads of your Archived data while it is still accessible.

After the submission, you will get an email from Facebook confirming receipt of your request.

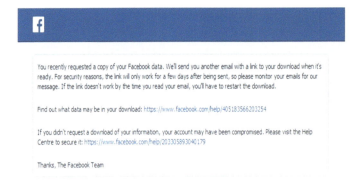

You will receive another email when your data is available for download. Click on the link in the email and you will be directed to your Facebook account with a page to download your data archive.

You recently requested a copy of your Facebook data. It's now ready for you to download.

Because this download may contain private information, you should keep it secure and take precautions when storing it, sending it or uploading it to another service.

Click the link below to go directly to your download. If the link redirects you to your account settings page, simply click "Download a copy of your Facebook data" to be redirected to the file we've prepared.

Please note: For security reasons, you can only download the copy we've prepared for you within a few days of this email being sent. You'll need to start the process again if you're unable to access your download.

https://www.facebook.com/dyi/?x=...&b=all_archives&referrer=old_job_finished

Depending on the software (if any) you have installed for handling zip files, you will get a prompt asking you what you would like to do with the download file which at the time of this writing comes as a zip file.

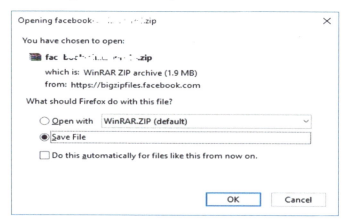

You can then unzip the files/folders into a folder using Extract To for WinRAR or drag them all into folder and double click on the index.htm file to see your data with Facebook.

3.4 Summary of steps for managing your data accessible to other apps from Facebook

i.   Go to settings

ii.   Go to Account Settings

iii.   Go to Apps

iv.   Go to Logged in with Facebook

v.   View the list of Apps

vi.   Select an App

vii.   Review the data access for the App, make changes and SAVE or click Remove app and confirm.

Happy "Facebooking"!